Deer Black Out

Deep Blackout

Deer Black Out

poems

ULRICH JESSE K BAER

Red Hen Press | *Pasadena, CA*

Book design by Luci Barrett

Library of Congress Cataloging-in-Publication Data

Names: Baer, Ulrich Jesse K, author.
Title: Deer black out: poems / Ulrich Jesse K Baer.
Other titles: Deer black out (Compilation)
Description: First edition. | Pasadena, CA: Red Hen Press, 2024.
Identifiers: LCCN 2023040161 (print) | LCCN 2023040162 (ebook) | ISBN
    9781636281520 (paperback) | ISBN 9781636281537 (ebook)
Subjects: LCGFT: Poetry.
Classification: LCC PS3602.A383 D44 2024 (print) | LCC PS3602.A383
    (ebook) | DDC 811/.6—dc23/eng/20231121
LC record available at https://lccn.loc.gov/2023040161
LC ebook record available at https://lccn.loc.gov/2023040162

The National Endowment for the Arts, the Los Angeles County Arts Commission, the Ahmanson Foundation, the Dwight Stuart Youth Fund, the Max Factor Family Foundation, the Pasadena Tournament of Roses Foundation, the Pasadena Arts & Culture Commission and the City of Pasadena Cultural Affairs Division, the City of Los Angeles Department of Cultural Affairs, the Audrey & Sydney Irmas Charitable Foundation, the Meta & George Rosenberg Foundation, the Albert and Elaine Borchard Foundation, the Adams Family Foundation, Amazon Literary Partnership, the Sam Francis Foundation, and the Mara W. Breech Foundation partially support Red Hen Press.

First Edition
Published by Red Hen Press
www.redhen.org

ACKNOWLEDGMENTS

Many thanks to the editors and readers of the journals where these poems originally appeared.

Deluge Journal: "Kintsugi Variations"; *Fruita Pulp*: "The Church of Cattle Entrails," "Deleuze Fucked My Mother"; *Horseless*: "Foreclosure Rodeo," '"Mareshiver",' "Pegasus, My Mother"; *Holodeck One* (Magic Helicopter Press, 2017): "Ana / Morphosis," "Beejar," "Holodeck One," "Stumping // Effects," "Tide Withdrawn Signal"; *Pinwheel*: "Mineralremitting::radioact"; *Prelude Mag*: "Deer Black Out."

CONTENTS

Horse ran there.
Desire.

    —Louis Zukofsky, "A"

Horse
is a crypt word, the rider another. Do go
somewhere.

    —Lyn Hejinian, *The Fatalist*

Deer Black Out

KINTSUGI VARIATIONS

Rilke's mother's fingers, deep
in pianosnow

Suicide Attempt I

Grass-trussed sex
scent of green

Suicide Attempt II: Dressage in Cabot Cove

Angela Lansbury: bowed white horse
my grandmother and I were awed by her
amble in grace

she is taking the Cavaletti
too fast

waltz in the shadow of a grisly murder
with her pencil skirt rubbing
her thick haunches

She has come here to resolve
the pastoral question:
woman.

Suicide Attempt III

Saint Judas

Suicide Attempt IV

I fucked him in the car
lick innerknee
thundercloud settling
rubbing to slickness
out of the dark

It didn't hurt.

Suicide Attempt V

Self-immolation: wildflower beam
from the nightpalm

Suicide Attempt VI

Dear Katie,

Everything is beautiful here and so full of blossom if I
could I would I am cattensile in the dream of a new life
when will you visit?

My scars are coming gold

THE CHURCH OF CATTLE ENTRAILS

Even before the abductions started,
cattle burrowed their pain
& we borrowed their cowbells because
there was a church, there was
no church, there was only
the mineral of the eyes

the fossil in the branch
tearing out

GRASSGRASSGRASS
GRASSa deer GRASS
GRASSGRASSGRASS

nothing was or wasn't
in it, nothing not of it
without knowledge we came
so loose that we
laid our cargo down
death hovered its saucers
& we were chasing there
was no church
only the following lights of the saucers

I wanted to draw up
through myself with that beam & visit
dead strangers who could conduit & crop
circles there was language
for conduits to come down

we were racing into amber
like murmuring prehistoric wasps there
was no church

there were schematics everywhere
which were hieroglyphs
which is what we are learning towards
as we nudge in the ground
they said their future was only image streams
dialectical starcharts,
because all diagrams are verbs
& predicates & vacant
they asked me what was sublunar
& how to tuck their bodies & tumble
if their ship caught fire in the sky;
they weren't under the same dictums

none of the ghosts knew
how to pilot their ship
were as if haunted themselves
by cloud memories
which are stronger than ours, more
purple than ours or compassed graves

they said they were
drones of the heart & weaponized
silence; they just wanted
to poke around
the cattle viscera
of a living earth, & probe meat they'd

forgotten how to feel
or what tenderness was like, flexing
against its tools or scalpels

they asked to borrow a fork
but I was already eating myself
it tastes good, I said, gnashing my mouthful of heart,
it was gritty; I was messy
with the ghosts
they didn't visit again, though we waited
were waited, there, where there was
no church to wait in

"MARESHIVER"

Quiverbranch
Sparrow song
in neck curve

kiss sweetness
from arch—rainflowering,
always mine

lilted rotation
ethereal spheres ravish
the un-ness of your

eye flare in silver
how to catch
each summering
moment

for you: choiring
sunflower field miles
ache
and are to rest

DELEUZE FUCKED MY MOTHER

My mother was a drunk:
Diverge, recirculate
in bedrock
My Mother died time & again
came back to
florescent weather
in the threshing-
machine

& curve back new-
brained / unroofed
asking for questions, all wrong
like, was whose
Body, in here? A turbulence?
Seraphim did my, sisterdeath?
I followed-path (geodesic) &
crow winged in
me, Mother?
It mottled round
cocksquamous /
process out
clumsy hooves, that
lived all figures

Now: brindled, Now: blind mirrored
I horsed along was, will not go it
again.

AFTER MARESHIVER

I.

Follow parabola horse incidence arching
Heaven for man promises
draw back
glittering pain-curve
repeat cessation in satiate

human is his tree
vault sky wind eat
over & over
sleeping out the leaves

distend grass mind
memorialize soil interior / anterior
man finite planetarium
of possibles

wound ground works
plinth sit in deaf
dust part dust
sea to cheek

terraflinch

bound up our earth

II.

planet fantastique
meadowmet
flower too much
petalpressures
rain slacks off

still holding raw down
cloud blown : pulped humus
touch rust nails memory

so far & further, remembering me,
remembering you were acred
by those hands holding
each another

III.

You were as deep
as water is in
the seed

when I took you, horseback,
thunder clattered horses
& moon-stepped
set silvering hooves
drenched us
waists turn though

IV.

Now   cattlepain
walks the land dumb

time's wheel herded
frost in the hart
I was a spot
on its back

shimmering deerlove
moves close by itself

V.

swallowearth

VI.

static planetary
stations

sets edges teeth

VII.

now gnash in

DEERONDEERONDEERONDEER
DEERONDEERONDEERONDEER
DEERINDEERWEINDEEEROONI
DEERFORDEERINDEERONDEER
DEERONDEERhurtDEERONDEER
DEEROFDEEROFDEERONEDEER
DEERUNDERDEERUNDERONEI
DEERONDEERONDEERONDEER

VIII.

The pasture can only mean death
for animal souls
buck

trample them
hoof for hoof

gladiolus arch-
angel plunge
through a mare
he had to be

mare / LIGHT

IX.

hoofrot : bridlerevolt

that they were climbing down

X.

I was the sand I was the shoal clashed shoal I was the
cracked flower I was the pebble I was the razor hidden
there I was the moistened I was the perish-logos I was the
horsewoman I was the bringing chaos I was the drowned
sailors rattling the chained oceans I was the rats clawing
the ropes above the rising swell I was the salt scattering
the lands I was the measure by which all things were that
I was

& then

X. Soften

When I wasn't a deer,
I missed the ruttling   through
your green
word.

BEEJAR

I.

You shoved in
that dense ear, its clustering
oscillated until I wasn't

a wave of flame, pushed
& pulled, this retreat
this anti-productive
hoofstep up to fire line

terra could rim
could glean its meat
from the the taut edge
head could rear, could storm

a circle, winding down
grass underneath grass
& nothing else there-tufted:
becoming, you were solely wet
ankles, arches graced
slendered nightjaw clack

bit ground, came up
pulped, guttered ravine
pluming its lucid mulch
fungus drives up

I took circumference
twice, twice flinched
elliptical desire to curve
& not break: the earth

the cantering earth, I took it
my horse was mouldered
my horsemeat was rotten
my horse skull was evolving
where were the eyes
who could give
me its eyes flashed
there, an immensity to fold to

horse she was unhorsed she wasn't
there was never a horses, there were
horse traps & pickets & so much horseshoes
little clamps inside her

brain, I rounded the gate, tossing you
flowers, you my petals, you my
petals to lose petals, & flaccid
bees, cumbersome with love
unspent, beecum up to their
beeeyes, that they could have them
when I couldn't, bee see
me yr smallest increment,
buzz.

II. Horsemeat

horsemeant, ensconced
sure bridle, hooved emergence
warmth

III.

Cliffs hangered
darkly hooded,
cliffs clamoring into
cliff more, the earth
waiting

IV. Dumbly

senses let go
dribbled semen
to dirtcaked

ease fluids out
yr stunted volume

You held nothing
but the gaze
held you back:
image stream

V. Noise

never last

VI.

Silence parlor
crystal swarmed canticles
light stuttered
growing more
emptied in

VII.

I meant it when I said I liked
you so much I wanted to
drive my car into a lake
signifiers drowned & we thought
they were just swimming out

Beach bonfire cinders rutting into sand
hurt sand clung its sharp, lies wedged
& there were so many words for fire
flicking matchsticks
lit or we left to lie

reside in yr mirror light devours
you too much alive
& smoke & smoke & smoke
heavy drag, relapse breath, lapse
in sand staggering waves;
their foam, limp
fractured

shimmer from it, still

VIII. Destaged

I found you
a trapdoor
exeunt from earth

the weed garden
all thorn & thistle & rasp
& fumblehands
& tumble to it
& tumbleweed back
unrolled too strong blue
edge pounded
mountain heightening
lashed its song
unlettered
to a thundercloud

IX.

Dreamed you into
its sound
its fractured sound
I drifted nimbus
away with these
hands : claws
filled in earth's crevice
a heart, a stillbeating

through fingers crease
three dimensional space
each face facing its dis-
appointment of depth
a lessness, a gull calling
the fish in its gullet
to debone its there
it's there,

we're there.

X. Thick Caulicles

& I never wanted
to come:
buzz.

TIDE WITHDRAWN SIGNAL

I.

Faltered schematics
chaffinch pulsate arbor
resound dapple
cusped de la mare trans
-literate
cold, swimming moons
of ideogram: pleated

polaris dismantled
rust frequency,
was all you could
go shattering as you
reentranced echolalia

I was swarmed by
you in ring of your own
pictograph, what was residue
reflected, thronged
out by us

II.

stars grappled bodies for progenitor
magma that could
define, ante-notes,
perfected in dissipation
movement we could mirror
& stretch thin to
muscle release a tonal mass

prefigured mass, in note
yrs sundered from its sea
& again

tide riffed harmonics
wrestle horizontal length
& widening in

green, yr expanse
faltered green, no
ground to be stood in
or up on, or for us

careen-step
toes web radial, pushed mud
dazzled pre-historical imprint
that you had talons before
fingers to touch me
my shadow

curling voluted to be
held by yr inchoate
curve purling to you
weightless

III. Schematics faltered

green in its hollow
trunk green past yr measure
devolving, green scuttled

a basin of mare-words, punctured
virulent syllables spilling through

my feedback circumference
of negation gnaws its own bones
what flesh couldn't
desire to lapse back

I coursed it
I, coarse, too
much rattled tape
phantasmagoric voice
in ectoplasm radiate mercurial
you shifted
modulate along my elliptical shade
or abscond, no roots
to tie earth up

IV.

perspective galaxy premonitory
allegory in divination : anastasis
slipped through
gutted fires

what might have been
a redolent God,
moraine horst, trample
hardened magma inside
stripped flowers
clip its pinion feather

wizened profile on loam: husk
of man, with seminal storm-eyes, cloud
in its cage, earth
scorched by itself

V. Repose In Form

where numbers race
their dissolution:
cloudcanyon

departed, yr stanzas
my withheld image of you
thins its swung moonlight

aurora borealis:
I struck deaf chords
when you grazed me
yr green
oscillated signals
recondite,

words are constellated
through yr lips
I can not cipher
my language,
whole.

PEGASUS, MY MOTHER

IV.

mother ambit
room w/o corners
that might crest or
catch a

mother double
bind, ogee rooted
tensile I was
in harmonics;
a bow plucked
me back over
myself tuned in
irresonant
as the blue
in a boulder.

V.

mother lyre, could it
love w/o extension of
a curve from which a sound

vibrate my reflection

this harmonic unremitting
interruption.

Tear yourself from.

FORECLOSURE RODEO

I.

Chrysalid
caracole horse
spurned index
fire's red & blue in
sides
shoveled ridges convergent
& breadcrumbling

palms leakyworld slipped
its face & cuffed
sleeves wrists turn out
rim to withdraw
or leave it

II.

music hears itself through / crystalips
pulpy massing behind yours,
& tipped shoal curve resounds
thick noised membrane terrawholly
I loam & moistened humus
black in default,
pre-rechording

II.

that brain recedes its swell
waves rearticulated parallax
& crashed up deboning
as mammoths crouched language

ice's share flashed mammothpain
or oiling wires
that trenched atmosphere's source
in violate barometric

a rain bow bellowed
death string univocal

where we were dressing in
each an other's fatality

& James Wright's horses
& bowing out

III. Gracefully

grass demures, or greencaging
landed vault to shaft
engendered its glasshead
rears of meadow
horseback arching
& graves ground through

a turf nudging
my prismatic powerful
obfuscating numina
stratified density

a nod headdirt
cradled teething beside
voluminous cock, earthyread
horseterror of empty
plunging infra red il
-legible

& marrow stood up
its combs calcified by heat
earths try to dusk
crepuscular muscle waning
& angels waxing
that knots barked up

celestial slide on friction
stars rasped to the socket
abscond a solareye, whets
of cold stone seas

a galactic brain
clanking its nails
& fanned across
exeunt in particle w/o
form

IV.

anchor residual
fossil ballast clavichord origin
cantata in terminus
spore extinguish light
seeds radiate null

repetition to recover
that hunched you, passed down
mountains careening
valleys humbled in shadowhums

a genetic litany
w/o hands, theos
leads storm behind
an unwheeled carriage

V.

a nursing home for horses
to fuck their way in
horseruined up the stable
& volcanic rubble clenching fist

a womb to scorch alveolusjesusinmountainprofile
where prancesong molts
& phase shift tines
a shape recalcitrant
as volcanoes were dynasties
& fuming ashen detextualized

a syllabary avenging angel
walled in

I or my was word broken horse trotted syllable for noise a steeple or fences took away
cowboys, molten horsefeathers extracting erotics bi-chorded a hammerhead horses
beating its dead wings against tectonic plates were tensile disagreeable even was the
first horse excursion when I horse selved that planes encompassed were ticked loose
or arrow gradual a diamond in the brain sparked I was all knees lapping pebbles
sharp clamshells when you full frontal assault of green

H   H
H H H H
H   H
H   H orseisgreen

blade experience picketed
& scout-teemed earth
where horseman post exited
a ledge spent archery
that no arrow could
be honest to land, science trim its
discursive, whereland

a method floundered   where were we picturesque ships & docked beaches
weighing on

unseen & blared fires
on the plain, no man was
alone

VI.

my mother was a
birdsilence asked me
to revisit pastures

& nightspread mantled
& dismantled
angels for horses
ecclesiastical fixtures
whinnying about it
or horse unshelving a sea

circuit show horses
I can not
do the rodeo
circuit again

HOLODECK ONE

I.

veery mountainbackside
trails off red/read shale
superpositions rock increate
horizon shyponied, quarries
mulish silence where up beast laps a line
man dance distance hollow
takes it to me, where eye
mise en abyme
mirror reslaughters it

treads "the
memory of
water"   A horse / man / ship
one, a face, its clipped rims, ground
less hangered into
me as sea
or star shadows wide
husked, sloughed ablack, pollen what
drifts in
fertile, the earthwomb
unsettles its green site
substratum extra
terrestrial reverberant
allparticled sound pre-rechording
grooves terrestrial & white
summits heightening strong
er than tetraktys must
\ mustn't

that you were woodslost
frenzied green, speaking wetness
into embanked shoal crust
stripping away there
like ideogram, sign ascendant, re
cedes, edges out, the maremouth
thick tongued dumb
or radiation prickles spinewhite
that planed movement
a modularity, or singular, pieces strike
back cardinal, yr immemorial back
sidle impossible histories sweep
the crevice of unfolding spine, or hand recesses
claviclechord, presses me up
song speaking one throat
from 2 mouths bent on lyres
aleatory alterity, each sequence
set to drown us in
the allnessnight
you my every
thing was moonwhere
trough it, the retina moon cunei
forms you pictogram
& diagrams lines up I can't re
course it

or forget again

II. like dust streams mountainbackside

letters
a fox trot dance
hall clods into dirt
horseline stepping floor
out to untouch halo
aurora redgreen cow
boy-boot, wordblack,
building image in
internal voice monument
steeltoed against measure:
remorse
full of trans
verse wavenoise, on
a taut wire I plucked
you blackteeth
& dismembering world
yr body too big to dis
junction

III.

Steeple
chase it

IV.

love's morphology

mercurial palms finger
less
tining skies miss
placed, different orioles
different songs now
words, now nothing but the
thing couldn't level
ground

an unseeded groove
we wind up
in two time
zones of experiential
holodeck, I'm ignition
here?

my holograph following shadow

this astral projection is deafening
the rust land, bluster stars as fossilized chants there
discants stratum lapsus, awaiting bare
cargo horizon, the terrain
memories water
foothold loess
uncreator eclipsing, evacuate celestial
spaceships drumming astralpulse
trajectory ashtrails a web in matrix of

erode yr face
into mine

world w/o a
face, noground horse's white
nosed green,
knows you
green

ANA / MORPHOSIS

Oar sea's ambergris
folded you under
& under
virgule sidereal
in the stammercorale
hurtless, rilling utter needles
petalspread by knee, shoveled circlecorpse re
parted lips a
round tree limn scrapes on
wherethunder
lambent grace arc
as misnomer double binds
recur
rent it

where you invented
flowers Gave
them to
flowers
shoots down bedrock
throes about
volcanic
or-age mulch

night tears it from you
you tear out a
way

cyclical Hemisphere if I
orbital re
monstrances, disre
membering

then
anamorphosis: He
virgule
She-process
bones mine out
white noise
that
InVeins?
residue a
Here

death instinct physoallegorical miss
under
standing you, tincloud
scraped pit, bitter holly
for hedgeworld, wearing at you
led one by reigns
knot down to the core
resound again

I / nightingale
thrashed in
Rockface poly
vocal rush leaf
oriole

Leitmotif
stringing body
impolitic eon
pinned to
love is paracrine

Chains to say I forgive
you prehistoric
Earthage rattling creek graved
turf where ghosthorsestreams
race number stations
we pass through them
as in them-thru-us

"Strips it
self naked"

what coal I
deveined, hands stained dirt
from the real
night tears it from you
white tree white branch
you tear out
away

STUMPING // EFFECTS

1.

that stumping corollary

2.

the real
transition down cloud
skeleton

3.

as birds in an unremitting land
scape
transistorized / unfinished

4.

that rebending, these wires
nexical sweep // electrical

5. schematical

form under
lying meadows

irresolvable of what
is meadowed   quality particular to

mise en abyme
the scene recurrence wave form

6.

How was affectation
all earnestness foots
bounding of yr eye
gouges green from
bud is hurt worse than a
not blossoming

movement
again

7. heavyheavyheavy

a gashed mountain
vein reticulated bloodsky
channels irrevocable
white in
side wind

8.

aleatory possible
semiconductor
insulatory boy / girl
exclusion

ahorse partition a
-temporal saddle circum
navigator waist groove white
thins electron?
cowboying resistor
to fences // an alterity exclusive
arcade vining a round sun
man is pierced up
on vault, where
wind tunnels
it again:
out of caverns, we
dawn bright & over
brimming

terrestrial
submerged peg of
man crumples the dirt

a rain
bow sound

9.

I plucked arrows out
yr chest herds winters in
graved
cowboy-it beams up
treading light arches
slowly in

10.

impossiblebirds

11. Genetrix earth mother

ship harmonic

you compose in, were composed
you :: chiasmus, chiral
delicately knees into
the bee hive, dripped
auto
erotics you
refrain

& intuit potential from thetree
to have been
loved messily thickening clouds
tumbled falling a
sleep way in
to dream modulated space ::
vacuum / continuum

infinite nest weaved
kingfisher or ocean—
blue deer
nudging the blue

antler that pathways
residue recurs.

as I in side
-real you
antiphonal
comets hurtled
replicated back term
-inate in beginning
us every bedrock
solid, space cove refirmed a
-new brain
to fixture
the still
life

In modules fluxive
yr sound returns them
to me // against the fence par
-taken cattle
raiders as
desperate imagos, the
stumping effect

Circuitwhere
a whole

pulse resists
it

the self / unfinished.

DEER BLACK OUT

Proto
gynic called deer black
out reverts to infra
red, my branches barren

or dualizing poles

where are my polarized ponies are you
as sweet as I remember you
always being

are you as transcendent
as you anamorph in
to shift less to form
I in habit my alien
body a bounds

the light leaky slopes at right angles
inter sects the cult cargo
strips it away

II.

I am the capitally
phase aligned sexual
-being petalnothing

these were technical terms
for a blandishment
as a bee scars
a membrane

& reticulates the green
I understood a gear
turns thru endlessness
of fragments,
compulsive

momentum of scattering
I blenderized in the stem
earthy whole :: hole mothery
we were just
scraping at pts
of overlap
the water traces
water / under / water
& nothing there left to leak
as a courage retrogresses
its chained to the center:
transitional phase

advection meant I couldn't
see you

this littleleast wrecks shore
of the skipping loop

juts out in rock
or clamors into
ash fans blanks out
cropping minerals
as we geminate differentials
unless more than
theoretical mien sky

glass abandons
in hollowing a chord
errant at the bow
-sprit the returnal circles
we align with a
derisive of elements
beginning at the mother
I can only charts
I can only
anti-gravity
& leaks at
horror's a vacuum   spectrum split out the lights
a radical number   of times division
beat partition race   horse anticipatory
& inchoate the ledge
where I strummed plenistically
the planes as
the plains as a mirror to dualize
I recurrent in to
the ground

III.

The circuit is in
the belike, belikened to
the ground

& shrugs itself sheer off
a scattering my leaf veins—gorges
& igneous theres hammered to
wetstone

to pulp humus
& trough at the
endlessness vines ware
out at the earth

& the horse
shot into
red holly, it is
mouth

my notes a sided a chord
that bit crusts & leave it
to foam always only
at the crease

IV. cleave

the alcoholic margins
never exhaust / myself

V.

I slump
shoulders under
to the phone lines
weight of twining inblossoms
refluent petals over
hung word
corners

MINERALREMITTING::RADIOACT

Proem:

Satellites, if you can come back
to the ellipse
you lapse in   the panoply
of forms, words'

I.

the brittleness green / fingers that tear
threads the roof / warped
b/t stations of form &
a content engenders

my grandmothers: in
side the harmonices—
angels that pull up

sentries
the forms-stations b/t
interstices:
the light crease in
a hand palms frond
and jute weather boxes
them,
that we make
trains, noise contours / of evocation
thrash parades: at last
confetti ultimatums
out lines the world
delimited an other

pass at time hands
pass them away

my deserts grown uncome
ly: husking thru

yr strange rays I keep
catching in to
flares at the pauses
breaks in—the feet
caryatid collapsing
structures a long shore
man architects
to himself: a glass
or the window when he
dyes the embroidered
turn the phrase in
to talons? We can't
equivocate w/ the
impartial fury of
nebulas: that its voice
constellate on & on
a spindle   needleseye
we weave & in
graft signs
my semiotics re
current & waves we
unsea being consciously
in descent of the draft
sign dislocates

my loyalty to forms
brambles thru, w/ these
mermaids: birdbeak
violence dips: its shoulder
a canvassed world
the sensorium pivots to

reclaim its oceanchord
we relict
our barrens
apart

to recreate

in the clay instant
uncome in

bells, & clanging down

my ladders
devolving
& the involutes
Endless when we
Crane in to fuse
Stamen stay
Human

Yr verses
Cowboys & the thresh
Holds the chaff

They elapse
An outgoing sign
Commandantes the west
Wetworlds I release
To a face
Not a fixture / we can
Have

Or I go away
As threatbirds: homing
The seas insolvent
Transmission
And mutating on
A vocable—light
Or the lower ranges
Where cattle prey
Birds we break their
Hands

.

II.

& no one is

III.

At home on the stage
Of referents we
Disband the nomen
-Clature rock shifts
In

& the hill
Locks—we valley away

IV. I'll have to

Lose the immanence
Of contents stumbled
Again we scrap
Heaps & love
I just inter / the limb?
Disjointed: a method
Of speaking into
Ligature—it
Flexs yr postulate
Back upon: the specular
Grounds a noise
We chain
Link w/ bars

I can not but
Submerge / I can
Not, but there

Last glances out
Side the gate:
Exteriors a carousel
& a fence scaffolds
Further & the garden
Drops behind yr green
Meteors recede—in
Audible

To resurrection:

I hulled
Meat—bodybags   is not / plow
Blades that plow bodies: epokhed
& we trundle w/ the
Blanks in the
Line dance, I careen
Into you—canyons? blood

What surfaces is
The machine
The thresher locked
In / to its throat
& choking on
Sound, it re
sounds

V.

I curve to
Bramble in
Tangle them

                                        Ponyshybowedinthe:lyre, reins
Meteors we un
Furl cords to / depart

VI. okeanos it

Sound
Waves relentless
So, I gesticulate
To retrieve my
Self—in the knot

-World climbs down
Making / unmaking
Clairtangents

& dominion: a range
The frontier is
Anger: I thrash
Back words
Again

Throne semiotic::handlesomatic
Much fissure in
Crease the lids
Rims lapped blue
Ourselves? Undid
The deer is
Blue terrestrial

rivers I transgress
The recurrency fluted
Wings nestled / the spine
Disfinger them
Colonnades horse is
done

VII. Broke-in

My arcades the last
Dance I tumble
True to position
Figures it fissures
Itself out
Side rain slants

The rest remains / itself

Buried

VIII.

Limbs you endjamb
The open: ends

& horsing
words, I act out
The Mountain ends
Mise en scene

Green throes down
Plains, I shrug w/

These: mt.s
babyteeth: & ridges
drown

w/ Horses, I ride
Them again

IX. voweloosened

satellites, in gods
arc we
intersect chains we
come down

X. as earth quarries to it / self

floodstepped
deer & we over

turn to minerals

GRASS BLADES

I. A diadem

Your fetid architecture
My staleness its cold
Outside—gone to tremble
In the unknown lands

I thought, if we could reach
A residual stillness, your mother is
There? We back off

Head—cuts them off,
we trundled our bed

Now dropped, the we
Instigative, the plural
I am going to
Have to lose

You, mountains, you
My gorges, my quaking
Folds part, to depart
To receive: you

II. in an eloquent sequence

I have not written

III. iowa plains, I would

Flatten

IV. enterregnum

I think the whispervoice
Has gotten too clawed up
My tonsils, stilted
With language too
Crisp the petal

You reenter

V. to lose your form

We quake

& in abandon
Meant meat, body/bags
To enclose you

VI. went off sauntering

Sidles his belt, fastening
Into immensities
We left off
At a ledge—word

You stumbled the hedge
Rows—doesn't break
With the waterline

Your bulking hulk
That busted up / on a dream
Foam, it drizzles

In the sky

VII. lit in pleine aire

Planes disembarked—the taxiing ranges

& saddle up to horses
Too tall you feel down
From the flexing re
Flexing breasts of
horses
Nuzzled you, bracketed
In the neck, so
Justlikechoking, so

an image under
Water, as mediums
We refract & the principle / is
Distortion, that translated you

Into cirrus language
Staggering to hold
Back:
Your throne

The night grows up molten

So refluency unends you

Were waterlogged,
Dog-eared, even stars tear
Out—& there was
A vista, to fold with
out

VIII. my madrigals

& the distance
Repeats

Until, the dust
Throats close

IX. & no aliens came to / or return

You don't re
Turn
The letter

& I keep foundering
With the crop
Circles, siloed inside

X. my face

A liquid border, it doesn't
Cross itself, when you
Angles, pass on

XI. the angels of the river

Pass on, I just
Founder

XII. with lines versus

Reverse us

XIII.

I amb, I amb

& don't ever wander

What you rake a way
Into, these grooves / where I make
My rust

Coasts rose in: patinaever

Bronzes, without voice
It enchants, & I go on
Deluding myself, but

Minerals can jut
Can take their lean
Into cliffs: another world

To clash like diamonds
In the dusk, we were
Dusked

& to you I bequeath

My last
Roses

Don't ever go forlorn

Jessica Baer you are
Immutable, later

To reform

Whatwhisperedtomewasthebedrock

Sheets in ice

Mammoth voices, pontificating
Until the late birds
Elide, cordstangled

In my mind

I blast eons, as arcadia
Relapse

Its contours, landescapes
Away from me

& the lyre, unends, I
A tone, & in its brevity
I will hold
You back

XIV. in duration

Later, I will align

XI. all my days

Were halcyon
& you nest
To your rest
Of time

XIV. grass blades, unreturned

from

AS DEER SKINS ITSELF

I.

sets
—emptying sound
exclosures
paddocks
-like
       articulate immensity
recapitulates   vestige

Chantey multi
ferous, idiomatic
motifs—recur

      uprooted idiom

II.

Rasp coppiced
fluctuate rhapsodic

Multiplexes illusive
Boundaries elude
Interstitial iterations
A marrow—suck
In space between
Grains

Logos spermatikos
Eon inchoate, its cycle
Complete

II. crash & crash

Sustained: harmonic
Sequence

Who elicit—
Snares

Clawed interior
Abstract never
The less   indefinite

Yelping

In which we begin,
          not with standing
Equipoise, posits
All the same
We tend   towards

Ichor restore
Orders   crystalline
Strong hold re:
doubt

Ligaments we are
bound for:

          rubbleseascapes

III. stag
grr'd
       glades abstract
words mesh
unfledged

       & back again
formation   dysmorphic

prefixes exact
preemption
      edenic over
turn

amorphic to
-gether

nominally what/we were
twins

VI. hunting for

the grounds—
terminal gardens
     stalk
-exhumed
      u symmetrically
      evr anthr

who succumbs:
mine   trophes

unaccompanied, it
is music still
here, exigencies

farmed fallow
form from fatcuts

a water shed
sidereal—the words
constellate prefaces
steep faces with
held light—

mutter permeates
hyperborean
forests no where

anaphora—syn
apses u stray

I gaze untendered
Kindling looks

Eons bear back
Predatory:
A heterotroph // marrow-sucked frm
the dead-does, the
trammel-caught   whom so studs

Pillage deer
Crests: furrows
Fledgling

Arrows ever an anther

What u u were
　　　　flowers
losing ur sap
　　　to

Meteors shower
w/ earth　　　absence
Hymnal　　　the celestial
Age　　a deer pelts
Skins it self w/
Feeling ur theme
recurs

SYMPHONIC REUNION

I. symbiotic reunion

fawns star eyed
we are surrogates
for the architecture
designed no hand
behind knowing

arterial arbor
vitae   tendril circlets
the living circuits
green grazed brash
animals din in
slips   the distance
oblique reentrance:
trespass tendril
millefleur, the gaze
pupae, ooze unshelled
when u

        you husked yr borders
slick w/ seed
pendant
crystalline structures
we dissemble
a fault line bind
carbon-stains
        yr here after

dendrites dangled
globular structures
music restrains them

from what? globes
protoplasm initiate
an amoeba reaches behind
neurology distends it
is losing—it shapes
the genetic drift a lovely
harmony away

seeds reside w/
the ens time
rhymes w/ the sending
letters down
to drown in a read
scree

     signalswhere
     cosmic
                we re eating the stars
                mountains bulge w/
u blueshifted
inviolate   frm me

to comb the forests
tresses scuzzed
with murk—water
swamps haunted by
symbiosis

in-moons   flower
yr zygote/happens to me

a stricken thing
     sloughed, it's armor

or it doesn't
transluce, yet

     a contingency means
     to touch u

once over always
undone

II.

     the problem with the psalm is that I am
       afraid to touch my self
     so I almost dont
     happen here   beside the edge
     the edges of time, saw u

combing the forest for predatory
verbs resound:
amalgamated stars

globular clusters
almost not our
selves, shapes strayed
forest lingers with red
meat. decay

under words' compression
we stoke time

anthracite contingent
upon burning   there

realized images
appear in ether
side—
ephemeral borders
where you were
volatilized

          pass into
          faces re

weave yr garland—
neural wreaths
the shadows you were
eclipsing in

immanence
deepends glades, the fires ravishing

who plumbs in
it   the crystalline
profile the fires
clearing   thins:signals

the ocean is
broadcasting longer than I can
          sfumato

shaved in tones
to me   yr reaching
incipient

evergreens u were shaded
nowhere

music breaks the air
cast to die
correlated with
reception   the godhead
vaults the set
plane of forces

magnetism's nascent
impetus in a body
heart chambers close
by itself   re - moving
worlds

enter a charred field
animals trembling
redounded
flesh fluxing

with sub atomic dust
yr fingers   sparkle
irretrievable, stars
their voices

yet, be yrself be
protoplasmic, pseudopod dawns

for man
-ifest the green
breaks & inter
the ruptures   the sum cedes
the biome
symbiosis ghosts trans
form
u, the blood trans
          fusion flares

for a circuit breaker, breaker
stalking the flesh
eaters the hyphae
touch embraced
world: here
u enter wracked with
dust

dream shades
haunted elisions
imperative to rust we
dismantled

whose world-ensouled
music, harmonies the spheres
rip away

from my vision—
          frm frthd frth

III.

elapsing prospective
words I close down
the picture show
images to animals

& moltenness grows   in the mirrorims
to overtake every
tree with ripening
clusters gone
orbs the stars
disordered terms

            the pastoral, still
            waiting

In u: face sulcus
echoes   between
cortex   stripped
wires yr timber
dissolved to
touch me

where else

            I strand in the music

gleans the ash
from fire crusts
of duration we stay
without culminant

forcesdusk lower
than the flowers
stirred ground
yr wires

meet me / if mother
ships harbor u can
raze yrself

      atoms

cluster'd grapes bronze
-hold branch the leaves
apart from me

      the sheer
      scale of loss

horses trample
valleys in grass

      no stations in the real
      midwest for mine

a progenitor wind
white cuts the alarms
flashing—
its currents demolish
me

in the channels,
you were flickering
          through

I overextended the
its music—throbs I don't know
why

the green builds   in yr statement, acts
disengendered
in the light
cane we catch on
stalks the fuming
worlds

at-orison
crest disks   blood
answers   interstice: the littlest
question I
forgot 2 seed
u go—
with the receding
perspective—

lines blur   below the tide

figures,   trans
fuse

          gazes the face
corners mine

when limns—stripd down
words gathered
the silt inside
yr faces bordered

rivers dont go
there any more

would you like to
live for
ever   vibrating between:
two vowels, the stars
fixed them & I
pursue its pulse
stamen stay
human trans
-duce

w/ does   the inGrass redress
yr sex   trussed fluid
albumen over run
the earth / paces in
what bull dozes
yr eyrie, I
evacuated

forms recondite—
transmit   a vacuum
sucks still the repulsed
satellites we fall
in phase

gauge away   & y cinder
centers compose w/
genetic drift   v lonely
litanies I
            untangle yr voice
birds throats—coincide   beside
mine—
an adit in
human shapes

fr u to come in
by verbs
to term again

fr u to come
reverb
to term them
again

fr u to come
to term
-inate again

fr u to come u
gestate to term
-inate them again u

tried / chords we never
severed

BIOGRAPHICAL NOTE

Ulrich Jesse K Baer received his MFA from Brown University in 2017. He was born in Georgia and grew up beneath Southern power plants. He has a poetry chapbook with Magic Helicopter Press (*Holodeck One*, 2017), a science fiction chapbook with Essay Press (*At One End*, 2020), and a full-length book with Apocalypse Party (*Midwestern Infinity Doctrine*, 2021). He has been included in journals such as *FENCE*, *Baest*, and *Bone Bouquet*. He loves horses and lives near Paris.

Printed in the USA
CPSIA information can be obtained
at www.ICGtesting.com
JSHW020935070224
56833JS00002B/3